**Ela Area Public Library District**
275 Mohawk Trail, Lake Zurich, IL 60047
(847) 438-3433
www.eapl.org

W9-AAT-592

31241010299561

AUG - - 2020

FAVORITE
CAT BREEDS

# BRITISH SHORTHAIR CATS

by Mary Ellen Klukow

AMICUS | AMICUS INK

Amicus High Interest and Amicus Ink are published by Amicus
P.O. Box 1329, Mankato, MN 56002
www.amicuspublishing.us

Copyright © 2020 Amicus. International copyright reserved in all countries. No part of this book may be reproduced in any form without written permission from the publisher.

Library of Congress Cataloging-in-Publication Data
Names: Klukow, Mary Ellen, author.
Title: British shorthair cats / by Mary Ellen Klukow.
Description: Mankato, Minnesota : Amicus/Amicus Ink, [2020] | Series:
  Favorite cat breeds | Audience: K to Grade 3. | Includes index.
Identifiers: LCCN 2018048903 (print) | LCCN 2018049066 (ebook) | ISBN
  9781681518558 (pdf) | ISBN 9781681518152 (library binding) | ISBN
  9781681525433 (paperback)
Subjects: LCSH: British shorthair cat—Juvenile literature. | Cat
  breeds—Juvenile literature.
Classification: LCC SF449.B74 (ebook) | LCC SF449.B74 K58 2020 (print) |
  DDC 636.8/22—dc23
LC record available at https://lccn.loc.gov/2018048903

Photo Credits: iStock/Nynke van Holten cover; Shutterstock/Paul_
Brighton 2; iStock/Helen Garvey 5; Alamy/Juniors Bildarchiv GmbH 6–7;
Wikimedia Commons/BritishEmpire 8; Shutterstock/Dmytro Surkov
10–11; iStock/Viorika 12–13; Shutterstock/Carlos G. Lopez 14–15; Alamy/
Galina Samoylovich 17; Shutterstock/Viorel Sima 18–19; Shutterstock/
Chendongshan 20–21; iStock/GlobalP 22

Editor: Alissa Thielges
Designer: Ciara Beitlich
Photo Researchers: Holly Young and Shane Freed

Printed in the United States of America

HC 10 9 8 7 6 5 4 3 2 1
PB 10 9 8 7 6 5 4 3 2 1

# TABLE OF CONTENTS

# ROUND ALL AROUND

A big, round cat watches birds. It has a round face and round eyes. Even its paws are round! It is a British Shorthair.

**Fun Fact**
The Cheshire Cat from *Alice in Wonderland* is a British Shorthair.

# GOOD HUNTERS

Long ago, Romans brought cats to England on boats. The cats hunted rats on the boats. Some of these cats were later bred into British Shorthairs. They are good hunters. They liked to chase things.

8

# ENGLISH CATS

These British Shorthairs were very popular in England. People loved their personality. The most common coat color is dark gray. This known as "British Blue."

**Fun Fact**
There is also a British Longhair breed from England.

# SHY AND SWEET

British Shorthairs can be shy.

They are **timid** around strangers.

But they love their families! British

Shorthairs are **affectionate**.

# COLORFUL COATS

British Shorthairs can be other colors and patterns. They can be **calico**, **tabby**, black, and more! They all have short, thick fur. It keeps them warm.

## Like a Wild Cat?

In the wild, snow leopards have thick fur, too. They need it to stay warm in cold, snowy places.

13

# COUCH POTATO

British Shorthairs are easy-going cats. They like to lie around. Sometimes they get a quick burst of energy and run around. But they are usually lazy.

# BOYS AND GIRLS

Boy and girl British Shorthairs

act differently. Boys are goofy.

They like to play. Girls are serious.

They prefer to cuddle.

18

# KITTENS

British Shorthairs usually have four kittens in a **litter**. Some look like their mom. Others don't. There can be many colors in a litter.

# A FAMILY PET

British Shorthairs get along with everyone. They are very **social** and love being around people. They even like dogs. British Shorthairs make good pets.

## Like a Wild Cat?
Lions are social, too. They live in family groups called prides.

# HOW DO YOU KNOW IT'S A BRITISH SHORTHAIR?

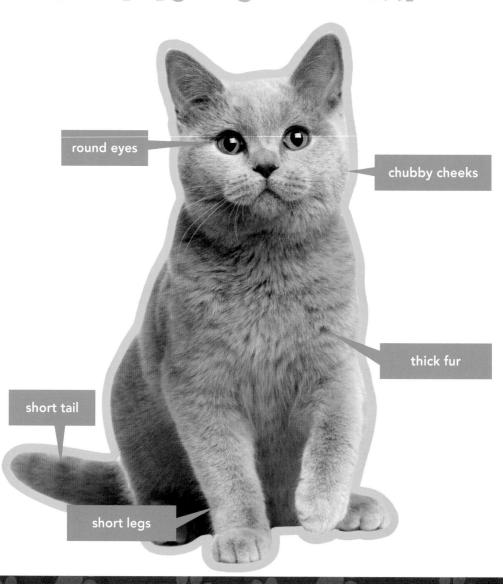

round eyes

chubby cheeks

thick fur

short tail

short legs

# WORDS TO KNOW

**affectionate** – loving, sweet

**calico** – white with black and orange spots

**litter** – a group of animals born at the same time to the same mother

**social** – likes to be around people or other animals

**tabby** – gray or brown with tiger stripes

**timid** – shy, a little scared

# LEARN MORE

## Books

Amstutz, Lisa. *Cats*. North Mankato, Minn.: Capstone Press, 2018.

Lajiness, Katie. *British Shorthair Cats*. Minneapolis: Abdo Publishing, 2018.

Leighton, Christina. *British Shorthairs*. Minneapolis: Bellwether Media, 2017.

## Websites

**CFA: About the British Shorthair**
http://www.cfa.org/Breeds/BreedsAB/BritishShorthair.aspx

**Science Kids: Cats**
http://www.sciencekids.co.nz/sciencefacts/animals/cat.html

# INDEX

Every effort has been made to ensure that these websites are appropriate for children. However, because of the nature of the Internet, it is impossible to guarantee that these sites will remain active indefinitely or that their contents will not be altered.